Washington
a photographic journey

photography by Tom Kirkendall and Vicky Spring

FARCOUNTRY

Right: A masterpiece in glass and steel co-designed by world-renowned architects Rem Koolhaas and Joshua Prince-Ramus, Seattle Central Library glistens at dusk in the heart of downtown Seattle.

Far right: Autumn announces its arrival as the larches turn gold above Colchuck Lake. Set in the Alpine Lakes Wilderness Area of the Wenatchee National Forest, this mesmerizing lake and its majestic surroundings are just outside of Leavenworth.

Title page: Since 1913, Point Wilson Lighthouse has guided mariners through the often-treacherous Admiralty Inlet, which connects the Strait of Juan de Fuca with Puget Sound. At fifty-one feet tall, the lighthouse, located in Fort Worden State Park at Port Townsend, is the tallest beacon on Puget Sound.

Front cover: Mount Rainier towers above the crystal-clear waters of Eunice Lake. The alpine lake, surrounded by fragile meadows and marshlands, is an awe-inspiring stop on the trail to Tolmie Peak or a perfect destination all on its own.

Back cover: Clouds and sunset converge beyond Crying Lady Rock at Second Beach, just south of the town of La Push on the Quileute Indian Reservation. This and other sea stacks and islets make up the Quillayute Needles, a breeding ground for birds and a national wildlife refuge. The sandy shore ends at a natural arch to the north and at the formidable Teahwhit Head to the south.

BACK COVER TEXT PARAPHRASED FROM
THE PRINCE OF TIDES BY PAT CONROY

ISBN 10: 1-56037-616-3
ISBN 13: 978-1-56037-616-3

© 2015 by Farcountry Press
Photography © 2015 by Kirkendall-Spring Photographers

For more information about our books, write Farcountry Press, P.O. Box 5630, Helena, MT 59604; call (800) 821-3874; or visit www.farcountrypress.com.

Produced and printed in the United States of America.
Printed in China.

19   18   17   16   15   1   2   3   4   5   6

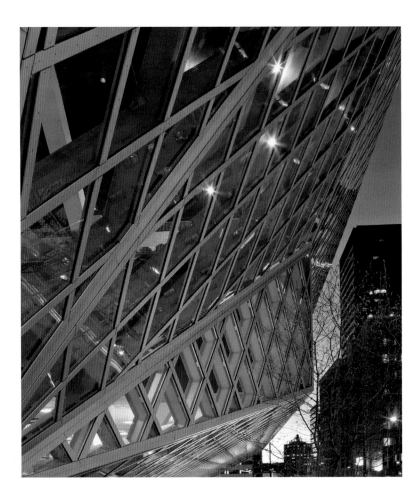

Far right: Sea stacks invite exploration at low tide along log-scattered Rialto Beach. This beach, in Olympic National Park near Forks, is perhaps best known for Hole-in-the-Wall, a beautifully sculpted natural arch north of here.

Right: A teenage girl selects strawberries at a U-pick farm in Arlington, which lies in the agriculturally rich Skagit Valley.

Below: The Palouse River cuts through layers of basalt at Palouse Falls in Palouse Falls State Park. These falls, the surrounding landscape, and the Columbia River Gorge were formed during the last ice age, when the Missoula Floods swept across eastern Washington.

4

Left: Artist's conk, sometimes called artist's fungus, grows on moss-covered trees along the East Fork Quinault River Trail in Olympic National Park.

Below: This sixty-foot Tlingit totem pole, stolen from its Alaska creators, was erected in downtown Seattle's Pioneer Square in 1899 and graciously reproduced by Tlingit craftsmen in 1938. The 1892 Pioneer Building, in the background, was headquarters for forty-eight mining firms during the Klondike Gold Rush of 1897.

Right: Seen from the slope of Steptoe Butte, fertile spring farmland rolls across the hills of the Palouse region in eastern Washington. The butte, a local landmark, rises to 3,612 feet in Steptoe Butte State Park.

Below: A truck waits for its next load at a grain silo at Oakesdale in Whitman County. The grain-growing areas of eastern and central Washington consistently put the state among the top five wheat producers in the United States.

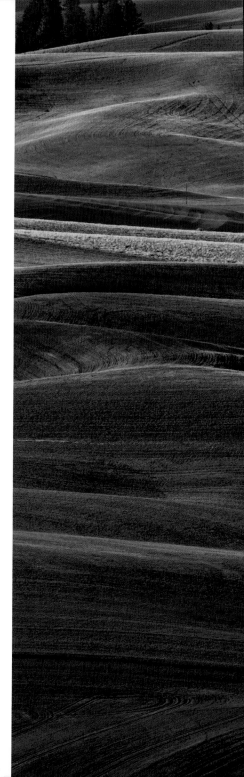

Far left: The Chihuly Bridge of Glass at the Museum of Glass joyfully connects pedestrians to downtown Tacoma. The 500-foot-long bridge features the *Venetian Wall*, the *Crystal Towers*, and the *Seaform Pavilion*.

Left: The Tacoma Narrows Bridge stands proudly between Tacoma and the Kitsap Peninsula. Only three months after its opening in 1940, the infamous "Galloping Gertie" snapped during a windstorm. The original bridge was completely replaced in 1950, and its twin was added in 2007.

Below: Countless train passengers were greeted by Union Station in downtown Tacoma over more than seventy-five years in service. After a decade of neglect, Tacoma revitalized this historic Beaux Arts building, now a federal courthouse.

Far right: Lake Union becomes a party playground as sailboats head out on the Duck Dodge in Seattle. The weekly race series has been held every summer for more than forty years.

Right: A climber scales a pinnacle called the Martian Slab in Peshastin Pinnacles State Park near Cashmere. These sandstone fins, some reaching 200 feet high, are accommodating to all climbers from first-timers to hard-core veterans.

Below: A backpacker boulder-hops at Moore Point along the Chelan Lakeshore Trail in the Lake Chelan–Sawtooth Wilderness. Getting here involves a ride on *Lady of the Lake* from Fields Point Landing or the town of Chelan—a journey that Lake Chelan vacationers have been taking for more than 100 years on the nation's third-deepest lake.

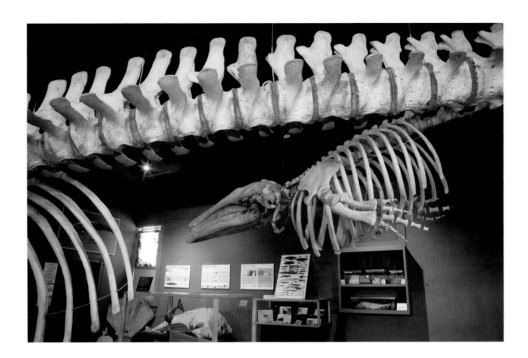

Above: Exhibits in the Whale Museum in Friday Harbor on San Juan Island offer a comprehensive look at local orcas and their pods. Along with its educational programs, the museum responds to stranded whale emergencies in the San Juan Islands in cooperation with the National Marine Fisheries Service.

Left: Just-picked Fuji apples are ready for transport to market. Washington produces about fifty-eight percent of apples grown in the United States on approximately 169,000 acres of orchards.

Far left: Built in 1908 by the Olmstead family, this historic farmhouse stands as testament to the lives of homesteaders such as the Olmsteads, who farmed this land after their arrival in the Ellensburg area in 1875. Their farm has since become Olmstead Place State Park, a working farm that demonstrates the life of pioneers in central Washington.

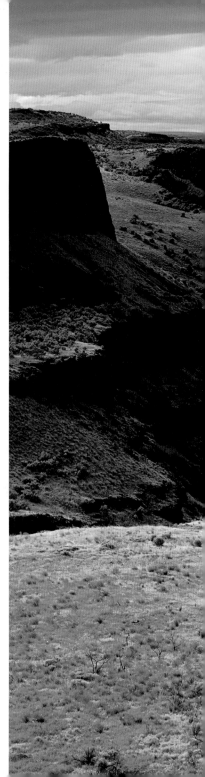

Far right: The Palouse River carves its way through Palouse River Canyon, showing off the basalt cliffs characteristic of the Columbia River Basin.

Right: Sulphur lupine grows on the open hillsides at Summer Falls near Coulee City. The falls are impressive despite being artificially created to allow seasonal overflow from Banks Lake.

Below: Seafood lovers dig for clams in Westcott Bay on San Juan Island. The bay has a commercial fishing farm, whereas the neighboring Garrison Bay is purely a recreational harvesting area.

Far left: The rich turquoise of Diablo Lake is a perfect canvas for the brilliant fireweed along the Sourdough Mountain Trail. The reservoir's color is the result of rock powder ground by glaciers. Colonial Peak rises abruptly in the distance.

Left: Native rhododendron, the state flower, adds a feminine touch to these restored barracks and officers' housing at Fort Columbia State Park. The fort was staffed from 1896 to 1947 and is one of the few U.S. Army Coastal Artillery Forts still intact.

Below: A mountain goat checks out who's checking him out at Colchuck Lake in the Alpine Lakes Wilderness.

Facing page: Downtown Seattle shines in the morning light, with Interstate 5 snaking northward through the heart of the Emerald City. Smith Tower, seen at the left with its pyramid-shaped upper floors, was the tallest building on the West Coast for almost fifty years. It is now joined by high-rises hosting a dizzying variety of prosperous businesses.

Right: The Edmonds–Kingston ferry docks in Edmonds to prepare for its thirty-minute passage, one of ten state-run ferry routes.

Below: The Seattle Great Wheel is a perfect place to watch the sunset along the Seattle Waterfront on Elliott Bay.

Above and left: Grand Coulee Dam—the largest concrete structure and largest producer of hydropower in the United States—harnesses the power of the Columbia River. Constructed between 1933 and 1941, the cultural, natural, and technological importance of this project is larger than the dam itself. The namesake of Grand Coulee's reservoir, Lake Roosevelt, President Franklin D. Roosevelt watches over the dam he championed.

Facing page: Lichen covers volcanic rock at Dry Falls Lake in Sun Lakes–Dry Falls State Park. The giant cliff of Dry Falls and the eroded terrain of southeastern Washington's Channeled Scablands speak to the immense forces of the ice age floods.

Facing page: Pike Place Market in downtown Seattle quiets down as evening settles in. Established in 1907, the iconic market continues today to be the place where farmers and crafters meet their customers.

Right: Crab pots and their brightly colored floats are ready for action at the harbor in Westport.

Below: A fly fishing rod and a handmade skin-on-frame kayak are the key to peace in the Strait of Juan de Fuca.

Left: This starlit campsite below Mount Baker makes for an enchanting evening in the Mount Baker Wilderness.

Below: Colorful rental kayaks are ready to slip into Liberty Bay on the Kitsap Peninsula.

Above: Washington State University's cougar emblem graces Martin Stadium in Pullman. The university opened in 1892 as an agricultural college and science school.

Right: An ochre sea star and sea urchins cling to the rocks in a tide pool in Olympic National Park.

Far right: This 155-foot clock tower is all that's left of the 1902 Great Northern Railroad depot, demolished for Expo '74 in Riverfront Park, located along the Spokane River in downtown Spokane.

Far left: A smoky sunset, the product of smoke from wildfires, blankets the Snow Lakes area of Okanogan–Wenatchee National Forest.

Left: Snow contributes to the Hoh Rain Forest's 140 to 170 inches of rain each year. Olympic National Park features one of the largest expanses of old-growth temperate rain forests in the United States.

Below: Bavarian culture is alive and well in the resort town of Leavenworth. Nestled in the Cascade Mountains, Leavenworth transformed itself into a Bavarian village in the 1960s to revitalize its economy. Today, almost 2 million people visit each year for a taste of alpine hospitality.

Right: Lupine and balsamroot go wild in the Dalles Mountain Ranch area of Columbia Hills State Park, while Oregon's Mount Hood towers above the Columbia River.

Below: Two of several pictographs and petroglyphs in Columbia Hills State Park near Horsethief Lake tell the stories of their Native American artists.

Above: A red barn is tucked shyly away in an apple orchard near Dryden in Chelan County. In the 1890s, when logging could no longer sustain the population, the community turned to apples to revitalize the economy.

Left: Fruit stands like this one near East Wenatchee dot the roads throughout the fruit-producing regions of the Wenatchee and Yakima River Valleys.

Far left: Sol Duc Falls plunges dramatically through the lush Sol Duc River Valley in Olympic National Park.

Far right: The Spokane River thunders over the falls and then under the Monroe Street Bridge in Spokane. The state's second-largest city, Spokane serves as the economic center of the largely rural and agricultural Inland Empire region.

Right: The historic Lake Quinault Lodge is just steps away from Lake Quinault, owned by the Quinault Indian Nation. Built in 1926, the lodge accommodated President Franklin D. Roosevelt in 1937. Nine months later, he signed the legislation that created Olympic National Park.

Below: Fragrance Lake reflects its dense shoreline forest in Larrabee State Park near Bellingham.

Above: Beacon Rock stands as it did when Lewis and Clark explored and named it in 1805. Located in Columbia River Gorge National Scenic Area, this landmark is the core of an ancient volcano. A one-mile hike leads to the summit, recommended for the incredible views.

Left: Larch Lake shows off its namesake trees in autumn, when the Chiwaukum Mountain Range of the Alpine Lakes Wilderness becomes a commotion of golden foliage.

Above: Less than an hour away from the bustle of downtown Seattle, fly-fishing on the Middle Fork Snoqualmie River near North Bend is a pleasant escape. All three forks of the Snoqualmie feature a variety of native trout species.

Right: Daffodils and blooming cherry trees signal spring at the Washington State Capitol in Olympia. Completed in 1928, the building's sandstone blocks were quarried near Mount Rainier at Wilkeson.

Facing page: North Head Lighthouse was placed on the northwestern spur of Cape Disappointment in 1898 due to numerous shipwrecks that occurred at the mouth of the Columbia River. The lighthouse is still active, now part of Cape Disappointment State Park on the Long Beach Peninsula.

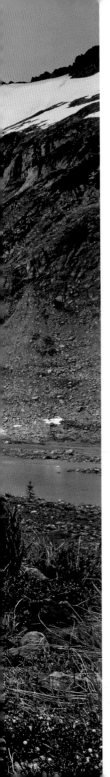

Above: It's said that true Seattleites won't carry an umbrella in the rain. Whether or not that's true, Seattle's best-kept secret is its beautiful, (mostly) rain-free summers.

Left: The fog over Grays Harbor begins to dissipate in the morning light.

Far left: Heather blooms defy the chill just below Lyman Glacier in Glacier Peak Wilderness. Washington boasts 3,101 glaciers, the most in the lower forty-eight states.

Next page: From Mazama Ridge in Mount Rainier National Park, Mount Rainier seems an arm's length away.

Far right: Katy Lake offers wildlife a place of respite in the Columbia National Wildlife Refuge. This small lake and others like it were formed either by ice age floods or by irrigation and reservoir seepage caused by the Columbia Basin Project.

Right: Emigrants traveled the Oregon Trail in covered wagons similar to this replica at the Whitman Mission National Historic Site near Walla Walla. The Whitmans settled here in 1836, leading the way to this site for as many as a thousand emigrants every year, some who just wintered and others who stayed.

Below: At Point Defiance Park in Tacoma, one of several Fort Nisqually building replicas helps to re-create the fort as it appeared in 1855. The fort was the first European settlement on Puget Sound.

Above: Deception Pass Bridge links the high rocky bluffs of Whidbey Island and Pass Island over the treacherous waters of Deception Pass in the northern Puget Sound. Canoe Pass Bridge completes the Highway 20 link between Pass Island and Fidalgo Island. Prior to the bridge's completion in 1935, the pass was navigated by ferry.

Left: The commanding officer's house still stands in Fort Simcoe State Park. Located on the Yakama Indian Nation Reservation in south-central Washington, the fort was established in the 1850s to ease tensions between settlers and Native Americans.

Facing page: The beach wilderness stirs the imagination at Cape Disappointment State Park. Cape Disappointment was named by English fur trader John Meares in 1788 when he was unable to locate the Columbia River.

Right: Docks line the waterfront along the Swinomish Channel in La Conner, located on the Skagit River Delta. Mount Baker holds court in the distance. Once a bustling port town, La Conner now attracts artists and nature lovers.

Below: A cross-country skier glides through snow-heavy trees near Snoqualmie Pass in the Okanogan–Wenatchee National Forest.

Far left: Dwarfed by one of the ferries it guides, the Mukilteo Light Station illuminates a distance of twelve nautical miles on Possession Sound.

Left: At 605 feet tall, the world-famous figure of the Space Needle commands the Seattle skyline from Kerry Park on Queen Anne Hill.

Below: The Space Needle appears to melt in its reflection on the colorful aluminum and stainless steel exterior of the EMP Museum, designed by Frank O. Gehry. The museum bridges the past and present through exhibits and performances that focus on cultural revolution, with a special emphasis on rock and roll.

Far right: Maryhill Winery vineyards thrive on the Columbia River. The Columbia Valley has the perfect climate and silt loam soil for producing wine grapes.
PHOTO BY GREG VAUGHN

Right: A formal English garden first cultivated in 1867 remains at English Camp on Garrison Bay. The camp was the British headquarters on San Juan Island when the United Kingdom shared the island with the United States. Today the camp is part of San Juan Island National Historical Park.

Below: Seemingly misplaced on a hill above the Columbia River, Stonehenge Memorial is dedicated to those from Klickitat County who died in World War I. Built in 1918 by tycoon Sam Hill near his Maryhill mansion, it is a full-scale replica of the ancient original in England.

Far left: Snoqualmie Falls crashes 268 feet on the Snoqualmie River just east of Seattle. Perched at the edge of the falls, the historic Salish Lodge was originally built in 1916 and was completely renovated in 1988.

Left: Cut logs await transport after being harvested in the Hoh River Valley on the Olympic Peninsula.

Below: Lupine carpets the hillside below the tower on the summit of Lookout Mountain. The 1962 fire lookout tower is one of the few such structures remaining in the North Cascades region of the Mount Baker–Snoqualmie National Forest.

Far right: Barnett Newman's 1967 sculpture *Broken Obelisk* stands adjacent to the Gothic-style Suzzallo Library on Red Square at the University of Washington campus in Seattle.

Right: A ferry prepares for loading at the Orcas Island Ferry Terminal. Orcas Island, like the other San Juan Islands, is accessible only via boat or airplane. Washington State Ferries is the largest ferry service in the country with twenty-two ferries and more than 23 million passengers annually.

Below: The Seattle Seahawks Blue Thunder drumline warms up with the team's famous 12th Man—Seahawks fans—on game day, a strategy that may have helped lead the Seahawks to their Super Bowl XLVIII win.

Far left: Tulips take over a commercial bulb farm in the Skagit Valley. Every April, hundreds of thousands of visitors tour the valley to be amazed at the colors. Skagit County produces more tulip bulbs than any other county in the United States.

Left: A topiary arch hints at the formal garden waiting on the other side. Duncan Garden is one of five gardens tended on the ninety acres of Manito Park in Spokane.

Below: Completed in 1912, Seattle's Volunteer Park Conservatory treats visitors to a bountiful selection of rare plants. This elegant Victorian greenhouse features five houses: Bromeliad, Palm, Fern, Seasonal Display, and Cactus. William Henry Seward, responsible for the purchase of Alaska in 1867, stands at the entrance.

Right: Beargrass makes its appearance at the base of Mount St. Helens in the Sawtooth Berry Fields of Gifford Pinchot National Forest. In designated areas, visitors may pick the delicious huckleberries that Native Americans have harvested for millennia.

Below: Built in 1876, the Cedar Creek Grist Mill continues its chore of producing flour and corn with its original power source: water. The working tour of this mill includes mechanisms both inside and outside the mill. The creek itself invites one to sit and ponder.

Left: A group leaves behind the skiing and snowboarding crowds at nearby Mount Baker Ski Area to snowshoe the open slopes of the Heather Meadows Recreation Area near Artist Point.

Below: Takhlakh Lake bears witness to Mount Adams presiding over Gifford Pinchot National Forest. Back roads to Takhlakh Lake Campground makes this a good site for accessing numerous trails, casting for rainbow trout, and paddling on the lake.

Far right: Mount Shuksan mesmerizes from the shore of Picture Lake, located in the Heather Meadows Recreation Area of Mount Baker–Snoqualmie National Forest.

Right: Nestled among the historic brick and concrete warehouses in downtown Tacoma, this ninety-foot-tall stainless steel cone fits in with the industrial landscape, but hints at the wondrous sights within the Museum of Glass.

Below: The original 1909 Boeing Airplane Company manufacturing plant, the "Red Barn" stands in a place of honor as a central part of the Museum of Flight, with exhibits covering Boeing's history from 1916 to 1958 in addition to the main building's thrilling overhead displays of aircraft from throughout history.

Above: A carver works on a totem pole. These poles are particular to Native peoples from the Northwest coastal regions through Canada and up into southeast Alaska.

Left: This old mill, likely the earliest flour mill constructed in what is now Washington, is an artifact left behind by the Hudson's Bay Company's activities along the Colville River near the town of Kettle Falls.

Facing page: The Twin Sisters rise above the sand dunes along the Columbia River near Pasco. The basalt columns, formed during the Missoula Floods, are a popular destination for hikers from the Tri-Cities of Richland, Kennewick, and Pasco, which thrive at the confluence of three rivers—the Columbia, Snake, and Yakima.

Right: Johnston Ridge in Mount St. Helens National Volcanic Monument offers an unobstructed view of Mount St. Helens. Much of the 1980 blast zone is visible, including the volcano's lava dome, crater, and pumice plain. Greenery on the previously barren landscape highlights the incredible recovery of plants and wildlife following the volcano's famous explosion.

Below: Bull Roosevelt elk graze in a meadow along the High Divide in Olympic National Park.

Facing page: Fishermen's Terminal in Seattle's Salmon Bay is home to the North Pacific Fishing Fleet. Located just east of Hiram M. Chittenden Locks, the bay's fresh water allows commercial fishermen to better maintain their vessels than saltwater moorage.

Below, left: The Sherman Pass Scenic Byway travels through some of the most remote and unaltered landscapes in Washington.

Below, right: Dusk settles on Point Robinson Lighthouse as the last daylight hits Mount Rainier in the background. This lighthouse sits on Maury Island in Puget Sound, about halfway between Seattle and Tacoma.

Far right: Snow geese fly over the Fir Island Farms Reserve Unit of the Skagit Wildlife Area. The reserve provides winter feed and rest for snow geese in the shadow of Mount Baker.

Right: The winemaker at Rulo Winery tastes an experimental lot of dry rosé made with pinot noir grapes in Walla Walla. Washington has more than a dozen officially recognized wine regions covering at least 43,000 acres of vineyards. PHOTO BY GREG VAUGHN

Below: Rainbow Falls competes for attention with the old-growth forest on the Chehalis River at Rainbow Falls State Park. This 139-acre park was established in 1935 a short drive west of Chehalis.